The
Xenophobe's Guide to
The Welsh

John Winterson Richards

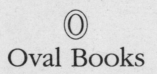

Oval Books

Published by Oval Books
335 Kennington Road
London SE11 4QE

Telephone: (0171) 582 7123
Fax: (0171) 582 1022
E-mail: info@ovalbooks.com

First published by Ravette Publishing.
This edition published by Oval Books.

First edition 1994
Reprinted 1996, 1997
Updated 1998
New edition 1999

PRPRT. HKGE NIDWANPRCHBD.

Editor – Catriona Tulloch Scott
Series Editor – Anne Tauté

Cover designer – Jim Wire, Quantum
Printer – Cox & Wyman Ltd

Contents

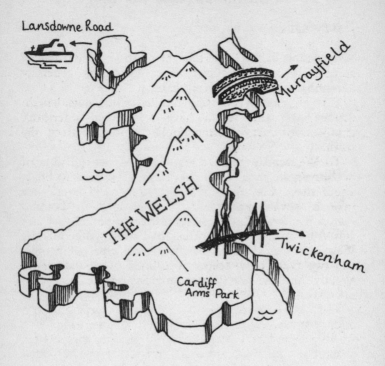

Lansdowne Road

Murrayfield

THE WELSH

Twickenham

Cardiff
Arms Park

'Rugby gives a tiny, impoverished nation the opportunity
to beat another with more than ten times the population . . .'

The population of the Welsh is 2 ¾ million (compared
with nearly 5 million Scots, just over 5 million Irish,
and 48 million English).

Nationalism and Identity

Forewarned

Some people like to boast that their nation is in some way superior to other nations. The Welsh are generally immune from that unpleasant habit.

This absence of boasting has led some outsiders to assume that the Welsh have a national inferiority complex. In fact, nothing could be further from the truth.

To Welshmen, the benefits of the wonderful gifts of Welshness are so obvious that there is no need to boast about them. Like true aristocrats the world over, they take the advantages of their birth so much for granted that going around telling others how superior they are would be pointless, and rather bad form. After all, the Welshman's world is made up of two types of people, and two types only: fellow Welshmen (who understand already) and the rest (whose opinions on the subject do not count).

This degree of national pride might be surprising in a poor, conquered, and exploited people, squatting on a small piece of harsh and intemperate land on the far edge of Europe – a land which is (greatest of insults) often mistaken for part of England.

One might well ask what the Welsh have to feel proud about. A Welshman could point out, in response, that the Welsh enjoyed one of the oldest and richest cultures in the world when the English were still illiterate barbarians (which was, according to most Welsh historians, not very long ago); that Wales was the cradle of British Christianity when England was a pagan wilderness (also not very long ago), and that the Welsh enjoyed the reputation of being among the fiercest fighters in Europe when the English were already weakened by soft living (about this morning). But none of that really explains Welsh pride.

This is because Welsh pride is real pride – the sort of mindless, instinctive, animal pride that requires no justification or excuse. It is simply pride for the sake of pride. Such pride is the only thing one has left when one has been stripped of everything else.

It is no doubt significant that this sort of pride is common to a number of impoverished and embattled hill peoples in different parts of the world – the Corsicans, the Afghans, and the Apache to name a few – and it is surely not coincidental that all of them have reputations for clannishness, deviousness, love of violence and vendetta.

How They Would Like Others to See Them

The Welsh simply could not care less what other people think of them. Among themselves, they not only think and believe that to be Welsh represents the highest form of human achievement – they know it.

Special Relationships

If the English did not exist, the Welsh would have to invent them. To a very great extent, the Welsh define their national identity in terms of the English:

"The English are X, so we are not."
"The English like Y, so we do not."
"The English dislike Z, so we absolutely love him/her/it."

Some people say that the Welsh have a love-hate relationship with the English but they are, in fact, 100% wrong. For a start, there is precious little love involved. Yet hate is also conspicuous by its absence which is surprising, given that the English conquered the country through treachery, killed its last native ruler in a particularly nasty manner, and, over a period of several hundred years, comprehensively looted its natural resources.

The Welsh attitude to the English may be more accurately summed up as 10% resentment and 90% pity. The resentment is not personal – it is a standard Welsh reaction to anyone who is, for any reason, better off (a Welshman will never accept that anyone can succeed where he fails without having some dishonest advantage).

The pity is also a standard Welsh reaction, in this case for anyone who has the incredible misfortune not to be Welsh.

The Welsh feel sorry for the English in the same way that a social worker would make excuses for a criminal from a broken home: "True, they did break into our country and steal everything they could get their hands on, but the poor things are English, after all." No doubt the English would be upset to find out how much the Welsh look down on them – which wouldn't worry the Welsh at all.

If the butt of a Welsh joke has to be effete, callow, pompous, ignorant, or generally substandard in any way, nine times out of ten he will be an Englishman.

For example:

First Welshman: "Excuse me, but you look like an Englishman."

Second Welshman: "No, I'm not English – I only look like this because I've just been sick."

The Welsh versus the Welsh

When they are not having a go at the English, the Welsh are having a go at each other.

For instance, in jokes about misers, the customary Scotsman is often replaced by the 'Cardi' – the inhabitant of Cardiganshire, a poor rural area where everyone is supposed to be mean.

Similarly, there is a tendency for the more cosmopolitan Welsh of the South Wales coastal strip to mock the people of the Valleys for a supposed lack of sophistication, and the people of the Valleys, in their turn, to mock the rural Welsh in the same way, this despite, or perhaps because of, the fact that most of the cosmopolitan Welsh originally came from the Valleys, and the Valley Welsh from the country, and not so very long ago.

This mockery is reflected in jokes about coal storage in bathrooms, outdoor plumbing, and the abuse of farm animals, especially sheep. And all that is in the single region of South Wales.

The different regions of Wales could almost be different nations. The North West, for example, is the most inaccessible part of Wales and so was the last bit to be conquered. Its people are most likely to be Welsh-speaking and nationalist. On the other hand, certain areas in the South are almost indistinguishable from England (Monmouthshire is actually shown as part of England on some old maps, and Pembrokeshire was known as 'Little England Beyond Wales').

There are lots of minor local variations, but the biggest contrast is between North and South. In general, North Walians and South Walians get on like a house on fire, the house in question having been bought by a South Walian and set on fire by a North Walian.

Each tends to see the other as a bunch of uncultured

primitives with silly accents, the difference in dialect between North and South Wales being as distinct as that between London and Newcastle, or Alabama and New England.

Needless to say, people from Mid and West Wales look down on both.

The truth is that the Welshman is only happy when he is part of an 'Us' having a go at 'Them'. It really doesn't matter which Us and which Them. Indeed, Us and Them can vary enormously according to context. It can be Wales against the world (or at least against England), one Welsh region against another, one district against another in the same region, one valley against the next, one village against the one down the valley, one local rugby club or pub darts team against its nearest rival, one street against the one running parallel to it, even one branch of the same family against another.

Two Welshmen who might be rivals in one context might be on the same side in another. For example, they may be fierce partisans of different rugby clubs but will cheer together when Wales play England, or their villages may have an antipathy towards one another that goes back centuries but will unite if it means getting one over those 'bastards' in the next valley.

Welshmen will put aside rivalries (temporarily at least) and close ranks in a most impressive manner when faced with a hostile outsider – but not always, for the tragedy of Wales is that the worst quarrels are often with those nearest at hand.

Wales was finally conquered because the last real Welsh prince had a dispute over land with some Welsh lords who joined with the English in the final campaign against him. They had forgotten that the whole point in having minor rivalries is to keep one's hand in when there are no outsiders around with whom one can have a major conflict.

The reaction of a Welshman to anyone who happens to be 'One of Us' or 'One of Them' at any particular moment is always extreme. One of Us can expect to enjoy every token of friendship, hospitality, and support, even if it involves a considerable degree of self-sacrifice on the part of the Welshman (he will treat a perfect stranger like a long-lost brother) but One of Them can expect no quarter.

When dealing with a Welshman it is therefore essential to establish One of Us status as swiftly as possible – and that is best done by finding some third party you dislike in common.

Behaviour

How a Welshman behaves towards you will depend on whether or not you belong to any of the groups with whom he is in conflict at that moment. If you happen to be in one such proscribed group, be prepared for anything up to and including single combat.

Some feuds are provisionally scheduled to last until the Day of Judgement, but others can be temporarily put aside in the interests of pursuing a common feud of greater importance. You can get away with being English when the British Lions are playing, or when the Welsh have just beaten the English at Cardiff Arms Park, at which point your Welshman will, in fact, become revoltingly affable.

In general, unless you are foolish enough to admit that you belong to one of those unfortunate groups, the Welsh are predisposed to be friendly.

Indeed, they can be very friendly, sometimes to the point of over-familiarity. Welsh travellers find it hard to comprehend places like the London Underground where people stare with almost frantic intensity at a point between their own feet or over a strange shoulder rather than run the risk of eye-contact.

In Wales, people routinely start talking with perfect strangers – on the bus, on the train, in the pub, even in the street – and not just about the weather. You can end up hearing the life story, complete with intimate emotional details, of someone you met ten minutes earlier.

There is very little reserve: the Welsh are a nation of compulsive gossips, and they enjoy talking about themselves. Any pretensions to social superiority will be cheerfully ignored. The Welsh are prepared, at very short notice, to talk to anyone as if he were their oldest and dearest friend, and they expect similar familiarity in return.

Elders

A partial exception is made in the case of senior citizens. The Welsh have a traditional respect for the idea of the village or chapel elder, and many Welsh people acquire with age the sort of dignity and gravity that would not be out of place in a High Court Judge.

When talking to such people, it would be wise – and indeed quite natural – to be as polite and as formal as possible. The response will probably be the usual Welsh one of extreme familiarity, after which you will be expected to be more familiar yourself, but the gesture of respect for age will have been noted and appreciated.

When a Welsh elder does descend to familiarity, as likely as not he or she will enjoy shocking you with

11

stories which prove that behind many a dignified old age lies a wild and turbulent youth. Sometimes one catches a glint in the eye which makes one doubt if they have ever really reformed.

Children

Children are naturally expected to run wild, and they usually oblige. The Welsh like children, and can be very indulgent, possibly because there is a touch of the Peter Pan about most of them.

However, there are formal occasions – church or chapel, big family occasions, etc., when children are brought out in their best and expected to behave with the sort of discipline that would do credit to the Welsh Guards – and woe betide the child whose behaviour disgraces its family in public.

Pets

The Welsh are generally less sentimental about pets than the English. There are some who are extremely fond of animals, but that fondness has a utilitarian streak. Animals may be loved but they must still earn their keep: dogs must work sheep or stand guard, cats must catch mice, horses and pigeons must win races, and, as for sheep, well, the less said the better.

Eccentrics

The Welsh are prepared to accept most people (unless in dispute with them) and most forms of behaviour (within certain limits). So they are generally fond of eccentrics, having quite a few home-grown ones of their own, as well as the English kind who give up everything to go and live in a caravan in one of the less accessible parts of Mid Wales. They are even fond of lunatics so long as they do not offend any common prejudices.

For Welsh people, the unforgivable eccentricity is to be successful. A poor eccentric will be the subject of sympathy and amused indulgence, but a rich one will be resented.

Outsiders

Although outwardly friendly to strangers in general, the Welsh are inwardly wary of Outsiders (i.e. everyone but blood kin), but, given time, their natural hospitality and familiarity will come to the fore, so most are relatively tolerant towards tourists and immigrants.

Indeed, the expansion of industry in South Wales in the 19th century attracted so many workers from outside Wales that the claims of many Welsh people to be Welsh do not bear close examination, so racial tolerance is a necessity.

Wales boasts some of the oldest coloured communities in Britain, many of whose members consider themselves, and are generally considered to be, as Welsh as anyone. The classic Welsh answer to discrimination by colour was given in the film *Proud Valley*. When a man objected to working with a black miner, played by the great Paul Robeson, it was pointed out to him that, at the end of the shift, Robeson's face would be no blacker than his own. Of course, Robeson's integration was helped by the fact that the man sang like an angel.

Yet no perusal of the behaviour of the Welsh could be complete without a consideration of a Welshman's relationship with the force that controls his life:

Wales' Best Kept Secret

Wales is run by a secret and sophisticated elite, the extent of whose power is carefully hidden.

Wales is, in fact, run entirely by women.

This will seem strange to an outsider since all the most important organizations in Wales – pubs, clubs, the Welsh Rugby Union, choirs, and, last and definitely least, the nominal government – appear to be dominated by men, but that only proves how clever the real rulers of Wales have been in concealing their absolute authority.

In reality, male domination of all those organizations means nothing because they are all simply a means of keeping the inferior sex occupied while the superior gets on with the serious business of running everything.

Consider this: the Welshman comes home from the club, his mind dulled by constant blows inflicted on him on the rugby pitch and by a few medicinal pints in the bar afterwards, and has to face a strong, sober woman who knows exactly what she wants. The poor man has no chance.

Welsh women are truly formidable. They are strong-minded and articulate, with clear objectives and absolutely no qualms about enforcing them. Welsh men are poor specimens by comparison.

The Welsh have a great military reputation as men who enjoy fighting and are good at it. This is probably because they found fierce and bloody warfare a pleasant and tranquil alternative to dealing with their womenfolk.

The dominant feature of a Welshman's childhood is his Mam. The traditional Welsh Mam is a combination of the gentleness of a saint and the degree of flexibility usually associated with the average mountain (and a Welsh mountain at that, formed of proper igneous rock – none of your sandstone rubbish).

Dad is a more shadowy figure, always 'down the club' or wherever (to get away from Mam), so Mam is the early power model and the young Welshman comes to associate women with power for the rest of his life.

With the sort of inevitability that a lemming would understand, he eventually marries a girl 'just like Mam' (nearly always the girl Mam tells him to marry), and spends the rest of his life 'down the club' – or wherever – where he meets and gets to know his long-lost father at last, while she gets on with indoctrinating the next generation.

Both sides are careful to keep all this hidden. In public, the Welshman will put on a big display of chauvinism when talking of his wife (usually, but not always, in her absence), trying to show his friends that he is a real man, in complete control of his woman. He convinces no-one, least of all his friends who are all also married to Welshwomen.

As the most amateur psychologist could tell you, such outward displays are a tell-tale sign of insecurity. Social convention may expect such talk, but the more extravagant and unbelievable it gets, the more you cannot help feeling sorry for the poor fellow as you realise what he's going to get when he goes home.

Manners

Welsh manners vary enormously. Most of the time the Welsh are fairly informal, but there are occasions when they can be excessively strict.

They have a great love of deflating other people's pomposity, but they also have a great respect for ceremony. They can go from one mode to another without a second's thought.

The same Welshman who will show the most perfect respect at a funeral may well be making humorous, even downright insulting, remarks at the expense of the deceased over a pint immediately afterwards. The trick is being able to judge the mood of the moment.

This can be very confusing. On Saturday night a Welshman might be completely smashed, singing rude songs, and mooning at passers-by on his way home from celebrating the rugby match. On Sunday morning on the way to chapel he is telling his children not to pick their noses.

Etiquette

Deep down the Welsh are a wild Celtic people on whom a veneer of Anglo-Saxon propriety has been forced by a powerful combination of Non-Conformist religion and Mam. The Welsh idea of 'manners' consists mainly of half-remembered scraps of English etiquette at mealtimes – "Don't eat with your elbows on the table", etc.

However, there are two rules of etiquette unique to the Welsh that must be followed at all times.

The first is that the correct response to any form of superior, social or otherwise (except, of course, Mam), is to show how totally unimpressed you are. This has led some observers to conclude that the Welsh have no class system. In fact the Welsh have an extraordinarily elaborate class system with a million tiny shades of distinction depending on family, occupation, and exact place of residence, but it is far too complex for an outsider to understand, and everyone is at pains to show how little it means anyway.

The second is that everything and everybody (except, of course, Mam) must be routinely and ritually made fun of, no matter how serious he/she/it may be; in fact, the more serious a thing is, the more it will be laughed at.

English managers assigned to Welsh factories often have difficulty coming to terms with the way that their workforces, far from holding them in awe as they are supposed to, expect them to stand their pint at the end of the day with everyone else and see everything they say as the basis for a joke.

Hospitality

There is one other aspect of Welsh manners which is quite distinctive – the Welsh tradition of hospitality. In Welsh history the guest was sacred. Once welcomed to the hearth, whether by a prince or pauper, the visitor, even if a perfect stranger, could expect the very best the household had to offer, and would be treated literally as one of the family.

In epic poems, great lords were judged as much by the hospitality they showed as by their prowess in battle, and poets often extolled in extraordinary detail the feasts provided by great men. To stint or hold back in any way was a matter of family dishonour. There are even tales of guests being revealed as the murderer of the host's father – usually the grounds for a bloodfeud for several generations – but being allowed to leave unharmed rather than offend the laws of hospitality.

The tradition survives today. If ever you are lost, homeless, or penniless, seek out the nearest expatriate Welshman, or, better still Welshwoman.

Character

It can no longer be concealed that this is, in fact, the second edition of the 'Xenophobe's Guide to the Welsh'. The original was published under the imaginative title *The Description of Wales* towards the end of the 12th century by a clergyman with the equally imaginative name of Giraldus Cambrensis which is Latin for 'Gerald of Wales'. It immediately made the medieval bestseller lists with at least three copies sold in its first century of publication.

Gerald was an early Welsh nationalist. The fact that he was only a quarter Welsh by blood, and that he had studied and established his reputation as one of the greatest scholars of his generation outside Wales, only seems to have made his patriotism all the more fervent (a common trait among nationalists).

His pet project was the establishment of a Welsh Metropolitan See, independent of Canterbury and England, with its own Archbishop. Unfortunately, by the time this goal was finally achieved, Gerald's favoured candidate for the post – Gerald – had been dead for 700 years, and that is usually considered a disadvantage when it comes to appointment to episcopal office.

It is a great pity that prejudice prevailed and Gerald never got the job because he really was a truly brilliant man. We know this because he tells us. He was the sort of man who could write lines such as, 'The word of God was preached with some eloquence by the Archdeacon of St David's, the man whose name appears on the title-page of this book, in short by me', and get away with it.

Good Points

Being neat of mind, he divided *The Description* into two books. *Book I* concentrates on 'The Good Points' about the Welsh. In it he notes with approval:

* Their respect for family.

* Their skill and courage in war.

* Their love of choral singing and of poetry.

* Their hospitality and generosity.

* Their sense of humour ('They love sarcastic remarks and libellous allusions, plays on words, sly references, ambiguities, and equivocal statements. Some of these are just for fun, but they can be very bitter').

* Their devotion to the Christian Faith ('They pay greater respect than any other people to their churches').

* Their natural acumen and shrewdness ('They are quicker-witted than any other Western people').

* Their 'great boldness in speaking and great confidence in answering, no matter what the circumstances, even in the presence of their princes' – unlike the deferential English.

Gerald has a ready explanation for the contrast between the English and the Welsh: the former have cold personalities because their ancestors came from cold Northern climes, but the dark colouring, 'natural warmth of personality', and 'hot temper' of the latter lead him to the conclusion that their ancestors must have come from the Mediterranean.

So far, so good.

Less Good Points

However, *Book II*, subtitled 'The Less Good Points', records:

* Their inconsistency, instability, and inability to keep their word, even when given on oath. This is why the verb 'to welsh' (meaning to go back on one's word) has entered the English language.

* Their unfortunate tendency to loot anything from anybody. ('It is the habit of the Welsh to steal anything they can lay their hands on and to live on plunder, theft, and robbery, not only from foreigners hostile to them, but also from each other.')

    Cattle raiding was a particularly popular hobby, especially along the border with England. The Welsh took great pride in it, and their poets wrote epics on the subject. The English also commemorated it in verse, but of a less elevated variety:

    'Taffy was a Welshman;
    Taffy was a thief;
    Taffy came to my house – and stole a leg of beef.'

* Their greed – at least when dealing with other people's property. ('If they come to a house where there is any sign of affluence, and they are in a position to take what they want, there is no limit to their demands. They will lose all control of themselves, and insist on being served vast quantities of food and, more especially, intoxicating drink.')

* Their love of feuding and vendetta. ('It is also remarkable how much more people love their brothers when they are dead than they do while they are still alive. They will persecute their living brothers until they bring about their death; but when their brothers die, especially when someone else happens to have killed them, they will move Heaven and Earth to avenge them.')

Finally, there was sex. Gerald, a clergyman sworn to celibacy, got quite heated on the subject. 'We see them still sunk in sin,' he wrote, 'and in a deep abyss of every vice – perjury, theft, robbery, rapine, murder, fratricide, adultery, incest.' He himself only got appointed Archdeacon after telling on his predecessor for living – apparently quite comfortably – with a mistress.

Stubbornness

The Welsh are stubborn – very, very stubborn. The Welsh themselves would probably rather say "tenacious", but to anyone on the receiving end a better description might well be "bloody-minded".

Gerald noted this when he described how the Welsh, even if defeated in battle, would come out ready to fight next day as if nothing had happened. 'They are very difficult to defeat in a long war', he observed. (He did not know how long: many Welshmen are still fighting the one the English thought they won seven hundred years ago.) In Wales even pacifists can be belligerent about their beliefs. Once a Welshman gets an idea – any idea – in his mind, nothing will dislodge it, and he will go to incredible lengths to realise it.

The Welsh can get some very odd ideas.

At their best, they can be visionaries, like the people who, for some reason, decided to set up a Welsh colony in Patagonia, of all places. Similarly, Welshmen have turned up signing the Declaration of Independence of the United States of America, acting as secret agent in Texas for the King of Spain, and rising from pirate to deputy governor of Jamaica (a feat accomplished by Sir Henry Morgan, possibly the most successful entrepreneur in Welsh history). Then there were those who went abroad, married well and founded a dynasty, most notably Owen Tudor who married Henry V's widow and fathered the best kings and queens ever to ascend the English throne.

Everywhere they go, the Welsh seem to display the most extraordinary opportunism – everywhere, that is, except Wales.

Extremes

If there is one thing at which the Welsh excel it is being excessive. Let Gerald sum up: 'The Welsh go to extremes in all matters. You may never find anyone worse than a bad Welshman, but you will certainly never find anyone better than a good one.'

They haven't changed.

Beliefs and Values

The Welsh like to believe, and would like others to believe, that they are bound together by a strong sense of community.

In reality, there is very little evidence of that in contemporary Wales. True, communities can come together in a very intimidating display of unity, but usually it is with the purpose of having a go at someone, be it a blackleg in a strike, a suspected wrongdoer who has not been dealt with 'properly' by more formal law, or, and best of all, another community.

What the Welsh really enjoy is being as awkward as possible. What they believe in, and value, is not being told what to do by anyone (except, of course, Mam).

Wealth and Success

This rugged individualism, combined with the natural cunning of the Welsh, and their skill at talking, should make Wales a nation of compulsive entrepreneurs. Yet in Wales it is considered almost bad form to better one's lot in life. The attitude to success, especially success in business, is one of extreme suspicion: 'He's no better than I am, so if he's got more than I have, he must have done something unfair to get it.'

Many Welshmen do rise above this prejudice and build successful careers in business – outside Wales.

There are a few so blissfully ignorant of national values as to succeed in Wales itself, but they are few indeed. As a result, most of the big employers in Wales have foreign bosses, giving the Welsh an excuse, if they needed one, to turn all forms of enterprise into another 'Them and Us' confrontation.

There are, however, some forms of distinction accept-able to Welsh sensibilities. Indeed, three things inspire positive respect: education, professional status and family.

Education

Working-class Welsh people have traditionally valued education as the instrument which would ensure that their children would not have to be working-class Welsh people.

Unfortunately, they have been a little too successful. The talented and educated young people soon realised that they could never make the most of their talent and education in a country where affluence is frowned upon.

So they and their descendants now live in the leafier suburbs of London, where they routinely complain of *hiraeth* (one of many untranslatable Welsh words, it conveys a longing for one's true home), but never return home for more than the briefest of visits.

Professional Status

This is seen as the ultimate goal of education. As far as the Welsh are concerned, there are only three proper professions: Medicine, the Law, and the Church. Teaching and academia, especially at University level, come a close fourth.

They have no time for the notion that modern professions like accountancy, surveying, engineering, or consultancy have anything like the status of the traditional

24

three, although they are quite prepared to boast about offspring who succeed in them.

This is probably a hangover from the miners of old who not only did not want their sons to follow them down the pit, but wanted them to get as far away as possible from the dirty business of production.

As a result, a disproportionate number of those who progress through education (often outside Wales) rise to the top of the medical and legal professions in Britain. It is quite possible to talk to an ordinary-looking working-class Welshwoman in her terraced house in a poor valley, and hear how her son is a successful barrister in the Inner Temple and her daughter is a consultant at a London teaching hospital.

Family

The centre of life in Wales is 'The Family'.

The Family used to mean the extended family including cousins to the umpteenth degree. Increasingly, it means the nuclear family with surviving ancestors, and those relatives with whom one happens to be on especially good terms, bolted on.

The reason for this is not a great social breakdown. Those who wax lyrical on the subject of extended families forget that they usually flourished because they were also neighbours. Families are now more likely to be physically dispersed and elderly relatives are less likely to live with the rest of the family. This is not necessarily a sign of neglect. It is more likely that the stubborn old girl refused to leave the Valley to live with her barrister son in Hampstead.

Big family gatherings are still frequent, and these are

important, almost formal, occasions. Christenings and marriages are good excuses for family get-togethers, but the most important is the Funeral.

Funerals are big social occasions in their own right. The Welsh talk about them afterwards and connoisseurs will judge them according to expense, organization, quality of eulogy, sincerity of grief, attendance, and venue, in the same way a Frenchman will judge wine.

Most Welsh people have an almost morbid fascination with the subject of death. Many will let themselves go short of necessities in their old age in order to save money for a good funeral – thereby probably hastening the day.

Class

The Welsh like to imply that they have no hereditary class system. In fact, Welsh history and literature exhibit a fanatical interest in family trees.

However, in Wales, good family has nothing to do with wealth or title. The Welsh know that all English titles can be bought for hard cash (it took a Welshman, David Lloyd George, to bring some honesty to the system by publishing a price list).

In any case, the Welsh have no need of paper titles when most of their ancestors could point to elaborately-forged family trees which connected them to all the famous princes and kings they could think of (a particular favourite was to claim descent from a fictional younger brother of Jesus). One exceptionally long and pretentious example is said to have a note in the margin about halfway through: 'It was about this time that the world was created.'

Most of the population is graded very subtly according to:

* Occupation of family members. Relationship, however distant, to someone of professional status confers standing, but all jobs have a greater or lesser degree of prestige attached to them. Some are finely graded, and peculiar to a particular industry or place of work: the difference between a 'Chief Assistant Engineer' and an 'Assistant Chief Engineer' might seem unimportant, but it isn't to a man who has worked for twenty years to rise from one to the other.

* Public reputation of family members. An international rugby player, a boxing champion, or a particularly strong Mam will reflect honour on the whole family; a quiet, unremarkable man will probably be an asset; but if a son or daughter crosses the invisible line between what can be tolerated and public scandal, the whole family is shamed.

* Place of residence, past and present, but especially where the family originally came from. One valley will be considered better than another, a village than its neighbour, one street than another in the same village, and even one side of the street than the houses opposite.

Marriage

In day-to-day life, none of this matters: the Welsh talk to each other freely without any regard to status. But if a marriage is in the offing, the older women who are the skilled judges in these matters will be making fine calculations as to who is marrying beneath themselves.

The draftsman's son from the Upper Village (whose uncle played twice for Wales, and whose grandmother was a fine woman) who marries the deputy night shift supervisor's daughter from the Lower Village (whose cousin... oh, dear) will soon have a fair idea of how the Prince of Wales would feel if he married a stripogram girl.

Apart from the importance placed on the relative status of the intending pair, the Welsh attitude to marriage has always been flexible.

Under ancient Welsh law women and illegitimate children actually had rights. This was considered a dangerous precedent by the rest of medieval Europe and was abolished as soon as the English took over the running of Wales.

Gerald became quite heated about the custom of living with a woman for a few years, possibly having children with her, before deciding to marry her.

Today this is as popular as ever. Indeed, the rest of the world seems to be following the Welsh lead.

Sex

In general, left to themselves, the Welsh have always been fairly free and easy on the subject of sex.

Gerald was shocked by how common incest was in Wales, and there are other forms of sexual behaviour which are so common that (whilst still considered wrong) they are treated lightly. For instance:

First Welshman: I hear Farmer Jones has been arrested for making love to a sheep.
Second Welshman: Really? Male or female?
First Welshman: Female, of course. There is nothing wrong with old Jones!

28

Or:

> Young Dai came home one day and announced to his Dad that he was going to marry Megan Jones. His Dad looked embarrassed. "Sorry son, you can't marry her. You see, a few years back, young Megan's mother and I were, well, very friendly, and, not to put too fine a point on it, Megan is your sister." Dai was extremely upset by this news. Later that day, his Mam saw him looking unhappy and asked him what the problem was. "I want to marry Megan Jones," he blurted out, "But Dad says he's her father." His Mam replied, "So what if he is her father? He's not yours."

However, the naturally passionate, and therefore tolerant, temperament of the Welsh was checked by the rigid morality enforced by the chapels. The two proved difficult to reconcile and the logical compromise for most Welsh people was to carry on regardless, but feel decently guilty about it afterwards.

The chapels didn't make the Welsh any less indulgent, but they did impose a thin varnish of 'respectability' on them. What people did was considered less important than what they were seen to do.

> *First Welshwoman*: Mary Pugh is getting married.
> *Second Welshwoman*: Is she pregnant then?
> *First Welshwoman*: No.
> *Second Welshwoman*: There's posh!

That conflict between 'respectability' and natural indulgence still dominates the Welsh attitude to sex. They know what goes on, and they tolerate it, but only so long as it does not cause public scandal – a sin the Welsh never forgive.

Religion

The Welsh used to have great respect for religion – of the Non-Conformist variety, naturally. With no peerage of their own, foreigners as their bosses at work, and the best of their own people seeking their fortunes elsewhere, it was only to the local Preacher that the Welsh could look for intellectual and moral leadership.

The chapels were the most powerful force for cohesion in Wales, but, typically, even they became an excuse for argument and division. Splits were common. There are lots of stories about how Mr and Mrs Jones leave the chapel because of theological differences. When the Preacher visits a couple of weeks later to persuade them to come back, Jones says that he cannot speak for his wife because they have since had theological differences with each other, and now worship in different corners of the room.

The point of the story is that it was not meant to be a joke. The following story is, but it makes the same point.

A Welshman was wrecked on a desert island. By the time he was rescued, he had built out of driftwood not only a house for himself, but a small town with a pub, a rugby club, and two small chapels.

"But why two chapels?" asked his rescuers.

"You see that one," he replied. "Well that's the one I don't go to."

Partly as a result of that attitude, the chapels have lost the position of moral dictatorship they once held.

But it would be a mistake to count Welsh religion out. Revivals are a regular event in Welsh history, and one can never rule out the possibility that another might be just around the corner.

Until then, the Non-Conformists have left a powerful legacy in the gloomy Calvinist fatalism that appears to weigh heavily on the Welsh. There seems to be a general feeling that nothing can be done to improve anything. This is closely related to the Welsh attitude to success. Whether it is a cause or an effect or both is open to debate, but the net effect is the same: a widely held belief that progress is both impossible and undesirable.

If the Welsh dwell on their past a lot, it is because they are prisoners of their history. However, theirs is an open prison that could not be run without the consent and co-operation of the inmates.

Obsessions

The Welsh are prepared to be obsessive about absolutely anything at a moment's notice.

They believe 'If a thing is worth doing, it is worth doing excessively'. The Welshman will have a severe identity crisis unless he is throwing himself wholeheartedly into something, ideally something which gives him an opportunity for a violent display of emotion.

The Welsh are particularly fond of showing their emotions since they discovered how terrified the English are of their own. So a Welshman will display his uncontrolled anger, grief or lust, even when he doesn't really feel especially angry, sad or lusty.

The Welsh are not really as emotional as they like to pretend, but they are a nation of compulsive actors.

They need little excuse for a lot of talk, always welcome for itself in Wales, with the additional possibility that it might lead to an argument which is even more welcome because it means even more talk, and could lead, in turn, to a bloodfeud. A Welshman will be ready to fall out with another at a moment's notice, over what is unimportant.

He is also expected to have strongly-held opinions on any subject, even if he never gave it a thought before. As was said of a leading Welsh politician, 'He is a truly brilliant man: he can talk on absolutely any subject for an hour – two hours if he knows something about it.'

Some of their enthusiasms are of a more permanent and general nature than others. The most important of these is for The Family – certainly almost all Welshwomen and the majority of Welshmen would put it top of their list of priorities and concerns.

However, any list (especially one drawn up by men) would also have to include Beer, Rugby, Singing (particularly by choirs), Talking, Arguing, and, ultimately, Feuding about politics, religion, or anything else that might crop up.

Some might also insist on putting a particular Club or Pub on that list, whilst others will stand up for traditional favourites like Chapel, the Welsh Language, Trade Unionism, and Poetry, which are now essentially minority concerns but which are generally respected as part of the fabric of Wales.

Finally, there is a plethora of local traditions which can also give the Welsh a chance to get worked up. In some areas there is a great tradition of competition between village Brass Bands. In others, Pigeon or Horse Racing flourish on the quiet (Gambling, it should be noted, is by no means uncommon in connection with these activities).

In the end, what you happen to be interested in or concerned about does not really matter to the Welsh. What matters is being passionate about it.

Leisure and Pleasure

Welsh leisure activities can be summed up very briefly: Sport, Beer drinking, Argument – with a bit of Culture and one or two other things thrown in.

Sport

The Welsh are traditionally mad about rugby.

Actually, it would be more accurate to say that the Welsh are mad about any sport at which they happen to be doing well at the time. More often than not, this means rugby. However, if a Welshman, or a Welsh team, happens to do well in anything – snooker, ice hockey, soccer, arm wrestling – almost everyone in the country will act as if they had been fanatical supporters all along. The day after a single Welsh athlete took no less than four gold medals at the Special Olympics, everyone was talking as if they had been following women's wheelchair sprinting for years.

However, rugby has always had a special place. The Welsh are traditionally mad about rugby. Rugby gives a tiny, impoverished nation the opportunity to beat another with more than ten times the population – and to beat it decisively and regularly. Rugby is the chance the Welsh have to humiliate the English at the game they invented. Rugby gives the Welsh their pride back. Rugby gives them revenge.

The Welsh are (normally) extremely proficient at rugby. They enjoy it and they take it seriously. This is because rugby – with its physical aggression, tactics, disciplined use of brute force and organized violence – is the closest thing modern day life can offer by way of Wales' traditional national sport: war.

The Welsh military scorecard is impressive: convincing away wins for the Welsh longbowmen in Ireland and France (Agincourt, Crécy, etc.), and some honour as part of a mixed team in Scotland (Welsh archers being the only part of the English army at Bannockburn which didn't break). True, they lost the series to England on a technicality after a despicable foul on the Welsh captain (involving the removal of his head) put him out of the game, but only after some solid wins at home and away. (It is, however, curious that Welsh victories like Leominster, Cardigan and Coleshill are rarely mentioned in English history books.) South Africa, then as now, was something of a bogey, but the points deficit at Isandhawana was decisively made up at Rorke's Drift.

Alas, rugby, like warfare itself, once open to all, is being ruined by professionalism. Wales is a small nation (in both population and average height) whose only advantage was enthusiastic amateurism. It is difficult to see how, in the long term, such a few poor, short people can produce teams to oppose larger numbers of taller people with the money to spend on selective breeding programmes.

Other regular favourite sports include boxing (because it can be almost as violent as rugby), and snooker, darts, and cards (because they can be played whilst drinking).

Beer Drinking

Welshmen drink beer. It would be accurate to say that Welshmen drink a lot of beer. This is confirmed by official statistics which consistently put alcoholic consumption per head in the 'Celtic fringes' – Wales, Scotland, and Ireland – above the UK average.

These figures, however, only tell part of the story because, if one excludes teetotallers (a higher percentage of the population in Wales where religion was often associated with temperance) and that proportion of any nation who prefer, for some reason, to remain moderate in their drinking, the consumption per head of the remainder of the population in Wales is astonishing.

It is recommended that an adult male drink no more than 21 units of alcohol a week (a unit is equivalent to half a pint of beer). In Wales it is by no means uncommon for a regular drinker to exceed this in a single night, quite casually and on a regular basis.

It is this casual attitude which distinguishes the Welsh from other nations with a reputation for hard drinking. It is simply assumed that any healthy Welsh male of mature age will be able to take his beer without complaint. It is therefore considered bad form to boast about one's feats of drinking – though if one happens to be given unsolicited praise a modest "I can't take it like I used to" is permissible.

It is also bad form to mock a man who cannot keep up. Yet, although formal drinking competitions are comparatively rare, in any gathering a Welshman's eyes will occasionally drop unobtrusively to check the level of his companions' glasses and if he sees he is behind, he will take a gulp or two to catch up.

It will also be noted if someone drops out of a round, and the phrase 'just a half' is frowned on in polite circles. Welshmen drink pints. Welshmen also drink in rounds. The round system is probably the basis of all social organization in Wales. The greatest sin in Wales (apart, of course, from supporting the English rugby team or disobeying Mam) is to try to get out of standing one's round.

Nevertheless, one of the most attractive features of the

Welsh is the way that, if a drinking companion is known to be seriously short of cash, there might be a sort of spontaneous collective amnesia about it being his turn to pay, or someone might offer to pay for the round jointly or make up the difference. There will be no fuss about the gesture and it will never be mentioned again. In that way a man might have both his beer and his pride. Since most Welshmen have been in that position at one time or another, there is nothing condescending in such an arrangement.

Drinking is a major national recreation. It is fairly common for a man to spend his leisure hours going to the same club or pub almost every evening after dinner and staying there until closing time. There is, therefore, no need for anything like the annual beer festivals seen on the Continent. For a Welshman, life is a constant beer festival. The nearest thing the Welsh have to a Continental beer festival is called 'The Rugby Trip'.

As a logistical exercise, preparation for a rugby trip puts D-Day in the shade. Whole off-licenses are emptied in order to load the coach with supplies for the journey. Seeing the cans stacked high on the seats, one might assume that the men expect to be away for a month until one overhears someone wondering if they have enough to get to their destination.

The test of the success or failure of a rugby trip is how much of it you can remember. If the whole weekend is a blank, then you must have enjoyed yourself.

Eating

Traditional Welsh dishes such as *cawl* (a delicious broth) and *laverbread* (rather nice if you can forget that it is made out of seaweed) are tasty and filling. However, in reality, more fish and chips, curries, kebabs, burgers, and Chinese takeaways than traditional dishes are consumed in Wales. These are the things that go best with beer.

Moreover, many catering businesses in Wales are run by Italians. The only food outlets in Wales which are not usually run by Italians are those which sell pizzas.

Clubs and Committees

The Welsh are big joiners of group activities – rugby clubs, political clubs, workingmen's clubs, choirs, chapels, and the social lives of many revolve exclusively around one or more of them.

Many Welsh pubs are so reliant on a tight-knit cadre of regular customers that they can also be viewed as clubs in their own right.

The Welsh are not by nature the most clubbish of people, but joining organizations offers them two things they really enjoy: the chance of rivalry with other clubs, and the chance of rivalry within the club. The latter is particularly important, for Welsh club politics make party politics look like a game for sissies.

Success demands a degree of ruthlessness that would shock the Borgias, and a knowledge of the subtleties of diplomacy that would not be out of place at the Byzantine imperial court. It also demands something which would confuse both Borgias and Byzantines: understanding the Welsh love of the Committee.

Why this nation of free-spirited individualists has such a reverence for the Committee can perhaps be put down to that part of every Welshman which enjoys formality and ceremony. Welsh committees are nothing if not formal. Any modern management theorist who tries seating a Welsh committee on comfortable chairs in a circle, getting the members to introduce themselves by their first names, and calling it 'the group', is asking for grief.

Business at Welsh committees, however insignificant and pointless it may be, and however violent the debates might get, must be conducted strictly by the book. This is probably only wise, given the Welsh propensity for both litigation and feud, and the tiniest mistake in a committee meeting could lead to both.

The Welsh can be very legalistic when they consider their own 'rights' are at stake. So a Welsh committee will be all "Through you, Mr Chairman", "Has the amendment got a seconder?", and "On a point of order".

To be elected to serve on a committee is seen as a high honour, even in organizations which have problems recruiting members. Yet the esteem in which a committee may be held does not prevent the membership of the organization as a whole disagreeing so vehemently with a decision its committee has made that a general meeting has to be held to overturn the decision and, possibly, to no-confidence the committee. This allows the whole procedure to begin all over again.

Culture

As they will be quite happy to remind you frequently, the Welsh enjoy one of the oldest cultures in Europe.

Most aspects of Welsh culture are of interest to hardly anyone outside Wales, and to precious few inside. There is, however, one honourable exception:

Singing

Singing is the one thing the Welsh are really, really good at – and they know it.

Choral singing is the jewel in their musical crown. The tradition, already strong in Gerald's day, was refined by the chapels that dominated Welsh cultural life in the 19th century.

Today's choirs can be strong social organizations in their own right, in the same way clubs are, but they are also made up of men who joined because they take their music seriously, and some are positively fanatical in their pursuit of harmonic perfection. The result can be heard. Welsh male voice choirs are simply the best in the world. The Welsh, with uncharacteristic modesty, admit that there may be music that is of greater beauty – but not on Earth.

Literature

Apart from singing, the most distinctive aspect of Welsh culture is poetry. Like many things Welsh, its poetry has a split personality: Welsh-language and English-language.

Welsh Language poetry has an ancient history in Wales (going back to the Celtic bards) and was very much an integral part of Welsh life. It also had a profound influence on European culture which is usually ignored by English scholars. It was the Welsh, for example, who developed what was to become the medieval romance, whose principal hero, King Arthur, was almost certainly a Welshman.

Welsh poetry is notable for its use of a broad vocabulary, and its emphasis on rhythm rather than rhyme. However, as Welsh-speakers will inform you with infuriating smugness, much of it is completely untranslatable because English simply doesn't have the necessary breadth of expression.

English-Language poetry on the other hand tries to exploit the Welsh poetic tradition without its greatest asset, the Welsh language.

Wales bred two poets of great renown in the English-speaking world, both called Thomas. They are easy to tell apart: Dylan was the Thomas who sometimes wrote nonsense when under the influence of alcohol, whilst R.S. is the Thomas who sometimes talks nonsense when stone cold sober.

Drama

The other thing that comes naturally to the Welsh is acting.

Given the propensity of Welsh people of all types to overact at every given opportunity, it is not surprising that those who manage to tone it down a bit have gone on to world fame as actors (or politicians, who are, after all, only an inferior species of actors). As with singing, no generation has been complete without a Welsh presence at, or near, the very top since Sarah Siddons (the 18th century's answer to Marilyn Monroe) was born in a Breconshire inn.

One name commands particular respect. The late Richard Burton was the Welshman's Welshman. It wasn't just That Voice: it was the fact that behind the voice was a man of obvious intelligence, passion, and character. The Welsh take a pride in any of their number who 'beats' the outside world, but, where most do so by hiding or suppressing their Welshness, Burton always seemed to remember who he was.

To see someone who was so clearly one of their own as a major figure in the glamourous world of the international movie star gave every Welshman a pride and a hope he never had before. To be Welsh was not to be condemned to a lifelong comedy-relief character part – it was to be a sex symbol.

The fact that Burton died relatively young after a life of heavy drinking and marrying beautiful women only added to his stature in his native land.

Custom and Tradition

The Welsh have many colourful and distinctive customs and traditions, most of which were invented by the Wales Tourist Board.

In reality, most Welsh women would not be caught dead wearing red shawls and tall black hats, whilst any young Welshman carving his beloved an elaborate wooden 'love spoon' would be better employed trying to earn hard cash to pay for a few good nights out and a van.

However, there are some genuine Welsh traditions, apart from rugby trips and family feuds, which still flourish. They include:

St David's Day

The National Saint's Day has always been popular, especially in those schools where it is a half-day holiday, partly because David is the only saint in Britain who actually came from the country of which he is the patron (Patrick of Ireland was possibly also Welsh, Andrew of

Scotland came from Galilee, George of England came from what is now Turkey), and also because he had the common sense to have his day on the 1st March which is an easy date to remember.

Welsh people are supposed to wear leeks on St David's Day in memory of the saint who lived on them to show his simplicity (and, considering his breath, his guaranteed chastity). Many now wear daffodils, not because they look prettier and smell less offensive, but on the rather feeble pretext that the word for daffodil in Welsh is similar to the word for leek.

The Eisteddfod

An *Eisteddfod* is the cultural equivalent of an athletics meeting, with competition in a broad range of artistic activities, especially musical performance.

The most important is the National Eisteddfod which is held every year in North and South Wales alternately.

Although proceedings are carried on exclusively in Welsh, many English-speakers attend, possibly attracted by the cultural elite of Welsh-speaking Wales dressing up in brightly coloured drapery and pretending to be druids, and the traditional ritual of Welsh-language extremists protesting violently against something and no-one doing anything to discourage them.

The Fake History of Wales

Welsh purists object strongly to the artificial customs and traditions created to promote a national identity. This dates back to the 18th century when the Eisteddfod, an historical meeting of bards dating from the middle ages, was 'revived' with all those unhistorical robes. The process was taken up enthusiastically by Lloyd George who cynically exploited Welsh national feeling for his own political advantage. It was he who 'revived' the Investiture of the Prince of Wales.

More recently, English bureaucrats thought it would cheer up the Welsh to replace familiar Anglicised county names (like Monmouthshire and Pembrokeshire) with 'revived' medieval Welsh names (like Gwent and Dyfed). It didn't, not least because the boundaries of the new counties had little in common with those of the medieval principalities.

However, these 'revivals' are only filling a gap left in the market because so many of the real customs and traditions of the Welsh have been lost.

The Real History of Wales

Considering the extent to which life in Wales is determined by its past, it is surprising how little the Welsh know about their own history.

They are not helped by the British history school syllabus and textbooks, mostly written by Englishmen, which hardly mention the subject and are especially silent on such matters as embarrassing defeats of the English by the Welsh, or the influence of Welsh culture on England and Europe.

More recently, 'local' history has been taught, but it is of the 'Social History of the Post-Industrial Valleys' variety that seems designed to convince most students their own national history is a total bore.

This is a shame because real Welsh history is stirring stuff. No boring lists of Acts of Parliament here, but tales of battle and betrayal, treachery and murder, ambush and escape, and even the odd true love story. In one two-year period of the Middle Ages, for example, one small district of mid-Wales saw seven killings, blindings and castrations, all of, and by, members of the same family.

Then there is the medieval Welsh response to unsuccessful property litigation. Two methods were developed, neither of which involved appealing to a higher court of law.

Method One pioneered by Ifor Bach ('Little Ivor'), involved breaking in to your opponent's closely-guarded castle, kidnapping not only him but his wife and infant son, carrying them out past over a hundred soldiers, and holding them hostage until they agreed that your claims had some justice in them after all.

Method Two, of which the most famous practitioner was Owain Glyndwr ('Owen of the Glen of the Waters'), was less sophisticated: you simply attacked your opponent's castle, captured it, and burned it to the ground – and then did the same to most of the other castles in Wales while you were about it. Both methods saved a fortune in lawyers' fees.

There was also the Welsh approach to domestic problems developed by Prince Llywelyn Fawr ('Llewelyn the Great') who is famous for killing people he found in bedrooms they should not have been in.

The first victim was his favourite hound, Gelert, whom he found in his son's room with a suspiciously bloody pile of blankets and no sign of his son. Jumping to the obvious conclusion, he killed the poor dog on the spot – only then did he find his son (alive) and a wolf (dead) under the bed, and was overcome with remorse when he realised his faithful friend had in fact saved the boy's life. He later found an Englishman in bed with his wife, and had him executed on the spot – but we may presume that on this occasion he had already checked under the bed.

Most of the villains of Welsh history are, predictably, English. The most reviled is the Baron de Braose, who invited a number of Welsh chieftains to his castle and then murdered them at dinner. Murder was all right, but the breach of the laws of hospitality was unforgivable.

The Principality

The constitutional status of Wales is deliberately confusing: it is part of the United Kingdom of Great Britain and Northern Ireland – but it is not itself a Kingdom. It is instead a Principality – or, as the Welsh prefer to put it when asserting their uniqueness, The Principality. This has two important consequences.

First, it gives a convenient excuse for not having the national emblem of Wales alongside those of England, Scotland, and Ireland on the 'Union Jack'. This is actually a flimsy pretext: the truth is that the Welsh dragon would look out of place among the neat crosses and saltires of the others – and would make the whole thing extremely hard to draw.

Second, the Queen is not Queen of Wales as she is of England, Northern Ireland, Canada, etc.

Historically, before its involuntary 'Union' with England, Wales was never a Kingdom – it was lots of kingdoms. Every lordling with four acres and a sheep (or four sheep and an acre) used to style himself 'king'. Eventually, the most powerful called himself 'Prince of Wales': this was interpreted as a diplomatic gesture of subordination to the King of England.

The gesture did not work, the Prince was killed, and his land taken by the mighty King Edward of England.

Legend has it that the cunning Edward then tried to placate his new Welsh subjects by promising to present them with a Prince of Wales 'who speaks no English'. He promptly kept his promise by presenting his own baby son and heir on a shield.

(In fact, legend got it wrong: the boy was a teenager when appointed, which certainly would have made it difficult for his father, big man as he was, to lift him up on a shield.)

Since then, 'Prince of Wales' has been purely a courtesy title, with no power or authority, borne by the heir apparent to the English Throne. Most of its holders have had little personal connection with Wales.

There is, however, an obvious advantage in having an Englishman as Prince: if the title were reserved for Welshmen, none of them would agree which of them should have it.

Crime and Punishment

The Welsh have one of the oldest codes of law, that of Prince Hywel Dda, 'Hywel the Good', a refreshing change from princes who liked to call themselves 'The Great'.

By the standards of the time it was extraordinarily liberal. It was therefore promptly abolished when the English took over and their great King Edward the Lawgiver decreed 'English common law applies in Wales'. The Welsh have been trying to prove him wrong ever since.

The tolerant and easy-going attitudes that characterise other aspects of their behaviour can also be seen in their feelings about law. They are all for any English law which happens to reinforce their own case in any litigation they are engaged in at the time, but otherwise they act as if the common law does not really apply to them.

Some offences are not taken particularly seriously. Fair fights between consenting adults and drink-related offences are often viewed indulgently, so long as no innocent third party is hurt, and bestiality, especially with sheep, is the cause of more bad jokes than outrage.

On the other hand, there are offences which so anger the Welsh that the law takes second place to mob 'justice'. Offences against the elderly and against children are firmly in this category, given the Welsh respect for the one and fondness for the other. Such mob 'justice' has a long history in Wales, and is not confined to those suspected of legal offences. Most of the police in Wales are local, so have the common sense to know that there is a time to be easy-going and tolerant, and a time to be strict, and which time it is at any particular moment.

Although relationships can sometimes be strained, the Welsh are generally comfortable with their police. Both share a horror at the increased number of mutually unacceptable offences (assaults on the defenceless, etc). Indeed, those who take part in demonstrations of 'popular justice' often do so because they believe they are helping the police out with a burden they cannot cope with alone. The police would really rather they did not.

Business

For most of its history, Wales has had a mainly agricultural economy. 'They pay no interest to commerce, shipping or industry', said Gerald. It was hardly an idyllic pastoral existence, but life went along happily enough.

Unfortunately, Wales had the bad luck to be rich in coal and iron deposits. When the Industrial Revolution put these commodities at a premium, people flooded into the Valleys where they had been found, not only from the Welsh countryside, but also from foreign parts (like Gloucestershire).

The Welsh prejudice against success ensured that most of the new industry was owned and managed by outsiders: there were Welsh supervisors and agents, but they were essentially NCOs under English officers. Welshmen did own or manage major heavy industrial operations – in the English Midlands, in the United States of America, and even in the Ukraine – but seldom in Wales.

As a result, when those heavy industries went into permanent decline, having ruined the environment of large parts of Wales, and having imported a large workforce and got it used to relatively high wages, not only was there little local business to fall back on but the Welsh people with the enterprise to create such business had been driven into exile for the crime of being enterprising.

The result was considerable poverty which had the comforting side-effect of confirming everything many Welsh people ever suspected about business.

However, this created a gap which has recently been filled by more and more European and East Asian (especially Japanese) companies locating a broad range of manufacturing operations in some parts of Wales.

The Welsh and these 'inward investors' (the standard euphemism for 'rich foreigners' in Wales), have found that they get on better with each other than either party does with the English.

For example, the Japanese practice of managers wearing the same overalls and eating in the same canteen as the men may only be a gesture, but it shows respect, which means a lot to people as proud as the Welsh.

On their part, the inward investors have discovered that the Welsh can be excellent workers if the passion they have for rugby and other obsessions can be inspired at work.

Doing Business

For all their negative attitudes to success, the Welsh actually enjoy the physical processes involved in doing business.

Three separate aspects of the Welsh character are brought together and indulged in the world of commerce and industry as nowhere else.

First is their love of talk for the sake of talk. The Welsh have always been born hagglers – a mixed blessing: industrial relations in Wales were traditionally about as quick and simple as the Thirty Years War.

Of course, business customs today are the same everywhere in the world – i.e. you do everything as efficiently as possible, or you won't be doing it for very long. Business in Wales now conforms to that international norm – but only, it must be said, after a heroic struggle on the part of the Welsh to suppress some of their most basic instincts.

It goes against the grain to do in seconds a deal which could more aesthetically be done after days of skilful dispute. Indeed, even today, give them half a hint that you might tolerate negotiation at length and they will consider it only good hospitality to oblige you.

Secondly, they make a point of positively enjoying the social side of business. Whilst it is now quite usual throughout the world to transact business under cover of a social event, the people of some nations feel under an obligation to make it clear that they engage in business entertainment because it is business, not because they particularly wish to be entertained. This is not true of the Welsh. They really do like a pint, a bite to eat, and a singsong, and if they can do a bit of business while they are about it, so much the better.

Thirdly, the most positive legacy of Wales' industrial past is a real fascination with technology. English managers and owners often saw the 'dirty end' of industry as beneath their contempt, but the Welsh have always had an interest in how things work: many employees had a knowledge of the technicalities of their industries that went far beyond the day-to-day demands of their jobs and would have surprised, even shocked, their employers; and much was picked up even by their families, and by neighbours who might not be employed in that industry but who depended on it indirectly.

Such technical awareness is therefore both common and respectable among the Welsh professional and upper classes whose English equivalents would probably conceal it even if they had it.

As a result, the Welsh are not unreceptive to new ideas. Most fads fail to catch on in Wales, but where the practical benefits of an innovation can be shown, the Welsh may mock at first, but will be swift to adopt, and possibly adapt, it.

The Welsh are nothing if not practical.

Systems

A great deal of money has recently been spent in Wales on highly visible improvements to various systems – new buildings, motorways, railways, rolling stock, etc. Enormous boards proclaim the virtues of the various public authorities whose generous funding enabled these improvements to go ahead, and a week rarely goes by without some initiative to better the lives of the Welsh people being announced in the press.

However, after all these well-meaning people have given their money, received their publicity, and gone home with a good conscience ("Hi honey, I'm home." "Hello, darling, how was work?" "Very satisfying – I dragged Wales into the 20th century today"), someone has to operate and maintain whatever it is they have so kindly provided.

This is when the real problems begin.

It isn't that the Welsh are lazy. On the contrary, properly motivated, their energy is astonishing, as has been proved on a thousand rugby pitches, in ten thousand pubs, and even in the odd place of work from time to time. The key words are 'properly motivated'.

Lack of enthusiasm prevents them maintaining the facilities at peak efficiency all the time. So the Welsh road system has some of the most spectacular new motorways in Britain, but it also has some of the most spectacular potholes in Europe. The Welsh rail system has brand new trains, but they are still as likely as ever to arrive late.

Moreover, concepts like 'Customer Service' do not come naturally to the Welsh because they smack of subservience.

Things are improving. The Japanese have been a positive influence, and the possibility of having better systems than the English is a powerful stimulant.

Shopping

There are two distinctive features of the Welsh shopping scene.

The first is the relatively strict observance of Sunday closing. This, like so much else, is a hangover from the days when the chapels ruled. In those days no-one would even have contemplated doing business on the Sabbath. Until recently, even the pubs in some districts were closed on Sunday – absolute proof of how serious it was to the Welsh.

The other is the survival of the old-style general store in places off the beaten tourist track. The breadth and range of products on display in these tiny shops would do credit to a department store – many are very old (from lines long since discontinued, or never even heard of), and have been on the same shelf for years, waiting for the day when a customer walks in wanting that very thing. You wonder how such shops can possibly make a living, but they do.

The absence of a Welsh product with a fashionable world reputation to give it a focus (like tweed and whisky in Scotland) is a disadvantage to the Welsh. However, many famous brand-name products are now produced in Wales, and they are beginning to exploit that. A campaign to promote 'Wales, Land of Quality' caused considerable amusement, not least among the Welsh themselves. They find it even funnier now that they stand a reasonable chance of actually pulling it off.

Health and Hygiene

The Welsh drink and smoke too much. They eat too many fatty foods. They suffer the diseases associated with heavy industries like coal mining, and the diseases associated with poverty as a result of the decline of those industries.

We are not talking about a healthy people here.

Their lungs have been weakened by coal dust and tobacco, their hearts by diet and tobacco, and their livers by alcohol. No wonder physicians are held in such high esteem in Wales. Yet the Welsh will respect their physicians but not listen to them, especially when they start dropping hints about giving up or cutting down on those things that make life liveable, like beer.

The Welsh view illness with their usual fatalism – it will happen and there is nothing to be done about it, so learn to accept it. Physicians do, however, have one useful function and that is to sign the 'Doctor's papers' that enable one to go 'On the Sick'.

In the days when much of the Welsh workforce was employed by the big nationalised heavy industries, it was accepted on all sides that everyone would be 'on the sick' on a regular basis. Indeed, in some places it was almost compulsory to take a certain number of days off sick every year – workmates would take a dim view of anyone who tried to show them up, and even the managers would be unhappy at the prospect of having their calculations upset.

Some of the causes of sick leave in Wales have yet to be adequately explained by medical researchers. For example, there is the virus which strikes down large numbers of workers every year at a time which happens to coincide with international rugby matches. An apparently completely unrelated virus often carries off distant relations at exactly the same time of year, necessitating the attendance at their funerals of those workers who escaped the first virus.

A number of Welsh work for Japanese employers, to whom the very concept is unknown. But the decline of the old industries has meant that, in some areas, large sections of the workforce are now 'on the sick' on a permanent basis. This is seen as an honourable alternative to unemployment from the point of view of both government and individual.

Cleanliness

The miners of old always found that, however hard they scrubbed to remove the coal from their bodies at the end of the shift, some would always remain. The same is true of the land. Nothing seems to stay clean for long in Wales. It is very disconcerting for those who spend millions on a bright, shining new facility to find that it has taken on a dirty appearance in a very short space of time.

Is it something in the air? Or is it the Welsh themselves? Certainly they do not have the inner compulsion for cleanliness, and the constant discipline required to implement it, that distinguishes nations like the Swiss. But they do have Mam, always a powerful force for order and propriety, who makes sure that when they do wash, they wash hard.

However, private cleanliness does not extend to public cleanliness. Perhaps this is another manifestation of their fatalism. If things are not clean, they are not meant to be clean, so nothing can be done about it.

The Welsh can be as houseproud as their English

neighbours, but the very fact that Mam is so tough about what is allowed in the home leads many a Welshman to treat everywhere outside as a place where he can dump rubbish, drop fish and chip papers, vomit, urinate, and let his dog do its business with impunity.

Government and Bureaucracy

The Welsh expect their politicians to be corrupt or incompetent or both. They are rarely disappointed.

Even those politicians who are fondly remembered in Wales are admired as much for their deviousness as for their achievements, the classic example being Lloyd George, who was a blatant hypocrite, but who is forgiven a lot in Wales because he proved that a Welshman brought up in the chapels could not only out-talk, out-drink and out-fornicate any Englishman, but also run the Englishman's Empire for him better than he could himself.

The Welsh – cunning, loquacious, and motivated by a love of vendetta and other people's property – are natural politicians. As usual, the best are generally exported. Those who are left often prefer the more competitive sports of family or club politics, but some actually seem to enjoy party politics.

Public life in Wales revolves around two main sources of power, both of which predictably involve a large number of committees: the Welsh Office and local councils. To these a third must now be added, the 'National Assembly', approved – with the usual degree of consensus in Wales – by a margin of less than 1% in a referendum. It is not yet known how it will work, but you can confidently predict it will involve committees.

The Welsh Office

This is the department of state of the United Kingdom responsible for Wales. It is headed by a Secretary of State who is a member of the British Cabinet and House of Commons.

The Secretary of State for Wales operates through a very large number of committees, known as quangos (Quasi-Autonomous Non-Governmental Organizations), most of which he appoints himself.

When, as is usually the case, the British Government and, therefore, the Secretary of State belong to a party other than the one most people in Wales voted for, opposition politicians like to call him the 'Viceroy' or the 'Governor-General', and compare the Welsh Office to a colonial government.

Local Government

Some local councils are legendary for their corruption. To be a member, at least of the majority party, is to be like a feudal baron, the centre of a personal network of mutual obligations, owing allegiance in turn to some higher-ranking baron, and treating certain perks of office as personal 'rights'.

Most astonishing of all is the almost cheerful openness of the way council houses, jobs, contracts, planning permission and licences can be assigned on the basis of kinship to, friendship with, or political support of, influential councillors.

While this level of misuse is not common to all Welsh local government, the Committee most definitely is. Every council has its labyrinthine structure of committees, subcommittees, and working parties. The Welsh reverence for the Committee is reinforced by the system by which the more meetings a councillor attends, the more he or she can claim in expenses, and the more complex the system, the greater the scope for manipulation. The cunning and ruthlessness required by Welsh committee politics come to the fore: Machiavelli would not last five minutes on a Welsh district council.

If all Welshmen are natural politicians, the best of them, the very shrewdest, are born public servants. It is not surprising that many Welshmen have gone far in the civil and diplomatic services, most of them, as usual, outside Wales.

Bureaucracy

Unhappily, the individual citizen with a complaint or an inquiry will not deal with these classy high-fliers, but with those nearer the bottom of the bureaucratic scale, where some of the worst features about the Welsh create the most unfortunate combination – their legalism and the love of form for the sake of form, their lack of energy in running any system for which they feel little personal enthusiasm, and, above all, their sheer cussedness.

For every action there is a reaction, so if the Welsh are bloody-minded when dealing with bureaucrats, consider how difficult bureaucrats who are themselves Welsh, and who have to deal with such people all the time, might be in return.

Welsh bureaucrats are like all Welsh people. Get them on your side, and they can move mountains for you; offend them, and you will be buried in more paper than Kafka ever dreamed of.

Politics

Welsh politics can be explained by this same desire to be difficult. Left to themselves, the Welsh are essentially a conservative (small 'c'), even reactionary, nation. However, in the 19th century, the Welsh generally voted Liberal simply because the English (who included most of their own bosses) generally voted Conservative.

Then, at the beginning of the 20th century, when the English (and the bosses) voted for a long period of strong Liberal government, the Welsh started voting Labour in large numbers.

Labour power in Wales grew with Conservative hegemony in England. The Labour Party's dominance of Wales is now so total that only one thing could undermine it – a prolonged Labour dominance of England.

Conversation and Gestures

The Welsh enjoy talking. They talk incessantly. They talk passionately. They talk about anything.

They also talk rather well. It is extremely common to hear well thought-out and informed opinions on complex subjects flow articulately, even eloquently, from an ordinary Welsh man or woman with virtually no formal education behind them. In Wales, more than elsewhere, it is foolish to judge by appearances.

Vocabulary can be surprisingly broad, and the Welsh have a gift for summing up difficult concepts in a single, neat, short, telling phrase, often delivered with the most beautiful grammar.

Two aspects of Welsh conversation can confuse

outsiders. The first is their habit of mocking what they hold most dear. The second is the way they argue most violently with those closest to them, because they know what they can get away with. A casual listener, hearing the raised voices and the name-calling of the most personal and insulting variety, might have difficulty in telling a normal discussion between good friends from the start of a bloodfeud. Sometimes, one or both participants have the same difficulty. But, more likely, within hours of the most vicious difference of opinion they will have forgotten all about it and resumed their usual pattern of friendship. This means they will be shouting at each other over something else.

Discussion in Wales is loud, emotional, and accompanied by violent gestures of the hands or arms. If a Welshman looks as if he is getting ready for a fight, he probably isn't. Earnest tones and quiet reserve have no place in a conversation in Wales.

Welsh Words

Welsh is a practical, as well as a poetic, language.

There are some Welsh words which neatly sum up concepts which would take a small essay to explain in English. For example, *hwyl* is translated as 'religious fervour' in some old dictionaries, but its meaning has broadened in common use. Today it conveys what might be described as 'that particular level of passion which can only be associated with the Welsh'.

Similarly, *gwlad* can appear simply as 'country' in dictionaries, but that does not adequately translate the depth of meaning the word has to a Welshman: when the rousing chorus of the Welsh National Anthem begins with a repetition of the word, it cannot be limply translated as 'Country, Country' – it is a strong personal affirmation of nationhood that goes beyond even 'fatherland' or 'patria'.

Welsh place names are less intimidating when you know that the Welsh prefixes *Tre-* and *Caer-* are more or less the direct equivalents of the English suffixes *-ton* and *-chester*, meaning 'town' and '[Roman] camp', respectively. The prefixes *Aber-* and *Ystrad-* have no short English equivalent, but the one conveys the point where river meets river or river meets sea, and the other a place on a valley floor. *Llan* – best translated as 'Church of' – is often incorrectly replaced by 'Saint' in English, sometimes in a rather bizarre manner: the English name for Llaneurwg (the Church of Eurwg) is Saint Mellons.

The famous Llanfairpwllgwyngyllgogerychwyrndrobwll-llantysiliogogogoch (the Church of Mary in the Hollow of the White Hazel near to the Rapid Whirlpool of the Church of Tysilio of the Red Cave) is strictly for the tourists: the Welsh, who are tired of the joke, use 'Llanfairpwll' or simply 'Llanfair PG' among themselves.

Keeping up With the Joneses

If a Welshman appears in a joke, he will probably be called Dai Jones (Dai is the diminutive of Dafydd or David, and Jones is the most common surname).

Given the poetry and imagination of the language, personal names are a disappointment. With their interest in family trees, it is not surprising that the Welsh were addicted to the patronymic: a man's father's name would appear after his own, then his grandfather's, and so on (until he got to the fake kings, princes and prophets) each linked by the word 'ap', ('son of'), e.g. Dafydd ap

Llywelyn ap Gwilym, etc. When English fashion dictated that they adopt surnames, most Welshmen simply adapted the names of their ancestors. Thus 'ap John' became Jones and 'ap David' became Davies.

Unfortunately, because many of their fathers had the same Christian names, a lot of unrelated people ended up with the same surnames – Jones, Williams, Evans, Davies, Richards. Since many also had the same Christian names, there was a need to distinguish between half a dozen David Joneses or John Williamses who might live in the same small village. The solution was a complex system of nicknames. Often they are based on occupation – 'Jones the Milk' and 'Jones the Post'. Sometimes a nickname may be a play on the name itself – a man named William Williams might well be known as 'Billy Twice'.

Language

It cannot be denied that Welsh is not an easy language. Except for Breton and the practically-extinct Cornish, it is like no other European language in grammar and vocabulary.

It also has a number of unique consonants. A nice Welsh accent, such as Burton's, can be smooth and melodious. A bad one can sound like Donald Duck.

Either way, the Welsh do try to sing the words, with changes of emphasis and flow, as they speak.

Even when speaking in English, they are influenced by the traditional forms of Welsh-language poetry with their emphasis on rhythm rather than rhyme.

Thus, when learning Welsh, you may ask what a particular word means and be told, "Well, nothing really, it just gives the sentence balance."

In the same way, when speaking English, a Welshman may end a sentence with a 'look you', a 'whatever', or an 'isn't it?' because, to him, the balance of the sentence seems to demand it. For the same reason, 'there' or 'by here' might be arbitrarily stuck in the middle.

Indeed, a large number of other English words might be used in the same way – sometimes at the same time. As a result, the English look down on the Welsh for not following the rules of grammar. They are wrong. The Welsh are following the rules of grammar, the ones that really count – the rules of Welsh grammar.

Similarly, a Welshman might say 'I am liking' instead of 'I like'. It may sound odd to English ears, but it is a literal translation from the Welsh, where the use of the verb 'to be' in that way is proper.

Although only about a fifth of the population of Wales can speak or understand it, the Welsh language is enjoying something of a come-back. More and more adults are learning it, some to rediscover their cultural roots, others, it is said, to understand the soaps on Welsh-language television.

There is a general feeling of goodwill towards the *hen iaith* ('the old tongue') among the English-speaking majority, but this is being eroded by two groups who create suspicion ('they want to force us to speak Welsh' is a commonly expressed fear) and even positive hostility.

The first is The Fanatics, the extremists who have given Wales a very bad press in Britain by burning cottages, defacing roadsigns, and vandalizing both public and private property, all in the name of promoting the Welsh language. In fact, their methods only provoke a reaction against the cause they say they are fighting for.

The second is The Taffia. It is now taken for granted among English-speakers that there is a conspiracy among the members of the Establishment who run Wales to promote only fellow Welsh-speakers to positions of power in all the important organizations in the country.

Of course, a good Welshman sees conspiracy everywhere. It is part of the 'Us' and 'Them' culture and provides a convenient excuse for his own lack of success – but it must be said that he could be right. Conspiracies of various kinds abound in Wales, and the Welsh-language lobby has an influence on policy far greater than its numbers would suggest.

If either of these two groups makes the English-speakers bloody-minded about the Welsh language (and they are just as Welsh as the Welsh-speakers so they can be just as bloody-minded) it could become yet another excuse for conflict.

It has to be said that a Welshman's accent in English is a poor guide to whether or not he speaks Welsh. Even the ability to speak Welsh is of itself a poor measure of Welshness. So is living in Wales, or having Welsh relatives.

Welshness is an attitude of mind – sometimes psychopathic, often generous, usually friendly, and always passionate.

The Author

John Winterson Richards has Welsh parents and was born in Cardiff, the capital of Wales, in no less a place than Saint David's Hospital.

Despite this most promising start, he turned out badly. It was soon discovered that he possessed a singing voice which would offend a frog, he enjoyed drinking French red wines even when beer was available, and the nicest thing ever said about his attempt to turn himself into a tolerably mediocre loose-head prop forward was that his 'enthusiasm for rugby greatly exceeds his skill'.

Obviously he was unfit for the company of civilised people. He was therefore exiled to England.

Whilst suffering this, the greatest punishment that can be inflicted on any Welshman, he got himself educated and studied to become a lawyer (being too lazy for medicine and completely unsuited for the Church). Living with the English for several years so broadened his mind that he became a rabid Welsh nationalist.

Finally overcome with *hiraeth*, he returned home and set up a management consultancy with the aim of bringing enterprise and prosperity to his fellow countrymen. Since few of them appear to be interested in enterprise or prosperity, he has had only limited success to date. This is probably just as well: had he actually succeeded, he would have caused far more offence than his singing ever did.